TRANSGENDER LIFE™

HEALTH ISSUES WHEN YOU'RE TRANSGENDER

SUSAN MEYER

ROSEN
PUBLISHING®
New York

Published in 2017 by The Rosen Publishing Group, Inc.
29 East 21st Street, New York, NY 10010

Copyright © 2017 by The Rosen Publishing Group, Inc.

First Edition

Library of Congress Cataloging-in-Publication Data

Names: Meyer, Susan, 1986– author.
Title: Health issues when you're transgender / Susan Meyer.
Description: First edition. | New York : Rosen Publishing, 2017. | Series:
  Transgender life | Includes bibliographical references and index.
Identifiers: LCCN 2016017416| ISBN 9781499464641 (library bound) | ISBN
  9781499464627 (pbk.) | ISBN 9781499464634 (6-pack)
Subjects: LCSH: Transgender youth—Mental health—Juvenile literature. |
  Transgender youth—Health and hygiene—Juvenile literature. |
  Transsexuals—Health and hygiene—Juvenile literature.
Classification: LCC RC560.G45 M49 2017 | DDC 362.196890086/7—dc23
LC record available at https://lccn.loc.gov/2016017416

Manufactured in China

Some of the images in this book illustrate individuals who are models. The depictions do not imply actual situations or events.

On the cover: Chalit Pongpitakwiset, a transgender male patient undergoing hormone replacement therapy, shows off his tattoo—the chemical structure of a testosterone molecule—outside his home in Bangkok, Thailand.

CONTENTS

INTRODUCTION

In *Beyond Magenta: Transgender Teens Speak Out*, a young transgender man named Jessy speaks about his childhood. He was raised by his parents as a girl and told to wear dresses. But even when he was six years old, Jessy didn't feel comfortable in dresses. He didn't feel like a girl at all. He wanted to wear a suit to the Valentine's dance at school. He resisted his mother's attempts to get him to take ballet, preferring to play soccer and take karate lessons. Plenty of young girls like to do karate and dress like boys, but Jessy knew he was different. He wasn't a little girl who liked to be like the boys. He wasn't a girl at all. Despite, what his family and teachers believed, he knew that he was a boy.

When Jessy went through puberty, like all teens, his body began to change. These changes made him both confused and upset. His body was growing breasts and becoming more feminine. He felt more and more at odds with his body. He knew something was wrong. It wasn't until Jessy was sixteen years old that he learned the word "transgender" from watching a television show. He learned that a transgender person's gender identity does not match the one they were assigned at birth. He immediately connected with the word and learned more about it. Years later, he would come out to his family with the news that

Transgender teens express their gender identity through their appearance in many ways, including how they dress and wear their hair.

he was transgender. Over the years, he also took steps to make his body more closely match his gender identity.

Gender identity and the way people express it is a key part of how they see themselves and how they interact with the world. Gender identity is the internal sense you have that you are a man, a woman, both, or neither. There are many different ways that transgender people may choose to express their identities. These can range from how they dress and style their hair to changes that require medical intervention—things like taking feminizing or masculinizing hormones and even undergoing surgeries. These are ways that a transgender person can, if they choose, make their physical bodies match their gender identity. Some of these procedures carry certain risks and side effects.

This book will look at some of the unique health issues affecting transgender people and transgender communities. Some of these issues relate to the procedures that transgender people may choose to undergo. Prior to these treatments, many transgender people may feel discomfort with their bodies, which can lead to greater emotional and mental health issues. Judgment from family and society can also cause stress, which can lead to other health concerns. Transgender communities experience higher rates of addiction, anxiety disorders, and depression. Their health and well-being is also threatened by anti-transgender violence.

If you feel that you may identify as transgender person yourself or if you are looking to gain information to be a supportive ally to a friend or family member, this book will provide important information on the health issues facing transgender communities. It will also look at some of the ways existing health care systems are difficult to access or provide inadequate care for transgender people, as well as the ways these systems are improving.

CHAPTER 1

WHAT DOES IT MEAN TO BE TRANSGENDER?

Humans are social animals. We like to form groups of similar people and to do that we also like to define ourselves with labels. In some ways, this is useful. It allows us to quickly make connections with people who are like us. In other ways, it is not so good. It can cause people to feel like they have to fit into only a few different choices or feel that there is something wrong with them if they don't. It can also cause other people to put labels on you in their effort to understand you. These labels may or may not actually represent how you see yourself.

For a long time, people thought that there were only two possible labels for gender identity. They thought that everyone had to be a man or a woman and that there were no other options. This is called the gender binary. Binary means having only two parts or, in this case, only two choices. We are now learning that gender identity is more complex than just two options. Identifying as gender nonbinary means that you don't feel like

This portrait is of a transgender woman. She identifies as a woman, not just in how she dresses, but in how she interacts with the world.

either man or woman really fits who you are. Nonbinary people are also sometimes referred to as genderqueer.

The word "transgender," sometimes shortened to "trans," is a term that is used to describe any person with a gender identity different than the one they were assigned at birth. People who are transgender may feel uncomfortable with their bodies, with the gender that many people see them as, or with the gender that is written on their birth certificates. They may feel their identity is male, female, or nonbinary. There are different words for describing transgender people that you may be familiar with. These include: genderqueer, transexual, MTF (male-to-female), or FTM (female-to-male). Some transgender people are comfortable with some of these words and others are offended by some of them. Feel comfortable choosing the words and labels you would like to use to describe yourself, but ask other people what they would like to be called. If someone is offended by a word you use, don't argue. Just stop using the word.

Another term you may hear in discussions of trans issues is "gender nonconforming." People who are gender nonconforming look or act in ways that do not fall in line with the social expectations of how people of the gender they were assigned at birth generally look and act. While the term "transgender" has to do with gender identity, "gender nonconforming" has to do with gender expression. While some people who are gender nonconforming are transgender, others are not.

GENDER AND SEXUALITY

Most people are familiar with the acronym LGBTQ. You may have heard it associated with pride parades and festivals, clubs or organizations at your school, or in the news relating to rights and

According to the Human Rights Campaign, 42 percent of LGBTQ youth say their community is not accepting of them. However, the same survey also showed that 77 percent believe things are getting better.

court cases. LGBTQ stands for "lesbian, gay, bisexual, transgender, and questioning." It's worth noting that some people define the Q in LGBTQ as "queer." "Queer" used to be a negative way that people referred to LGBTQ people, but has since been reclaimed and is often used by members of the LGBTQ community in a positive and affirming way. However, some people are still offended by the word, so if someone asks you not to use it, respect their wishes.

Breaking down the acronym further: you are already familiar with the definition of "transgender" and how it relates to gender identity. Lesbian, gay, and bisexual are not gender identities but sexualities, also known as sexual orientations. Gender identity is not the same thing as sexuality. A person's sexuality is whom they are attracted to and whom they have relationships with. A lesbian is a person who identifies as a woman who is attracted to other people who identify as women. "Gay" is used to describe anyone who identities as a man and is attracted to people who identity as men. Both gay and lesbian people are considered homosexual. Bisexual people are attracted both to men and women to some degree. Heterosexual, or straight, is also a sexuality. Heterosexual people can identify as male or female, and they are attracted to people of the opposite gender. Like gender identity, a person's sexuality can be an important part of how they express themselves and how they interact with the world. Although it varies greatly from person to person, sexuality usually develops much later than gender identity. Gender identity is established as early as toddlerhood, while people may not become of aware of their sexual orientation until early adolescence.

LIVING IN A CISNORMATIVE WORLD

You might or might not think much about your gender on a regular basis. Many people take their gender identity for granted. For example, your parents might have raised you as a girl since birth. Everyone in your life may now see you as a woman, and you may feel that being a woman is a fundamental part of your identity. People whose gender identity matches the one they were assigned at birth are called cisgender. Cisgender is the opposite of transgender. For transgender people, there isn't an easy correlation between the gender they feel describes them and the gender other people see them as. Their parents may have raised them in a completely different gender from the one they identity with. This can make them confused and frustrated, especially if people in their lives refuse to see their true identity.

The prefix "cis" derives from the Latin for "on this side of." The word means the opposite of "trans," which comes from the Latin for "on the other side of." While many people are familiar with the word "transgender" and have some idea what it means, fewer people are familiar with "cisgender." This is because a lot of

CISNORMATIVITY AT THE DOCTOR'S OFFICE

If you are used to navigating the world as a cisgender person, there are things you may take for granted that can cause discomfort for a transgender person. One of these is a visit the doctor's office. Accessing health care can be difficult for transgender people in part because not all doctors and health care professionals are trained in understanding their needs.

Before a patient even makes it to the see the doctor, they are given intake forms to fill out. Often these forms will include a box to check for gender: male or female. Not everyone's gender fits neatly into one of these two boxes. Medical history questions also make certain assumptions about a patient's gender identity. A doctor may assume that a patient who identifies as male will have the same health needs as any cisgender male.

Health care professionals can help improve the experience of their transgender patients by making forms that are more inclusive, thus allowing patients to not feel boxed in by choices that don't represent them.

cisgender people don't think to define themselves as cisgender. After all, their gender is visible to everyone and no one questions them about it.

Many aspects of our society operate under the assumption that everyone is cisgender. That kind of behavior is cisnormative. There are many examples of cisnormative attitudes in our world. You probably encounter them every day. Public rest rooms may assume that everyone fits neatly on the gender binary and offer men's rooms and women's rooms without a unisex option. There are even states that have passed laws to make it impossible for transgender people to use the public bathroom that fits their gender identity. For example in 2016, North Carolina signed a bill into law that would force transgender people to use the bathroom of the gender that is written on their birth certificates, even if that

Protesters in North Carolina spoke out against HB2, also known as the "Bathroom Bill," which would force transgender people to use the bathroom of the gender on their birth certificate.

isn't the gender they identify with. Such laws are discriminatory against transgender people, and many people spoke out against the North Carolina law.

The pronouns people use are also often cisnormative. Transgender people may choose to change the personal gender pronouns that people use to refer to them. They might stick to well-known pronouns like he/him/his or she/her/hers. There are also gender-neutral pronouns that some transgender people use, such as zie/zer/zir or ey/eim/eir. A good rule of thumb if you are unsure what pronouns people would like to be identified by is to ask them.

HOW DO I KNOW IF I'M TRANSGENDER?

If you are questioning your gender identity, you might wonder: How can you know for sure if you are transgender? There is no one answer. However, just by asking the question, you are likely experiencing some confusion about your gender and the way people perceive you. "Transgender" or "gender nonconforming" may be labels you want to use to describe your experience, but how do you know for sure?

Consider how you feel about your gender identity. Do you feel uncomfortable when people call you by gendered pronouns? Do you feel uncomfortable with the gender role that has been assigned to you or feel the way people expect you to act and dress doesn't fit you? If you have experienced or are experiencing puberty, is your changing body a source of discomfort and confusion? Do the changes feel wrong?

Another good place to start is to research other people's experiences. Read the stories of transgender teens describing their experiences and how they felt about their gender roles

Puberty is a time when many transgender youth start to question their gender identities and look for new ways to express not only their genders but their unique selves.

versus gender identities. Sometimes reading someone else's thoughts and experiences is the best way to have a moment of clarity and realize someone else out there has had the same internal struggle that you have. It also may be helpful to discuss what you are thinking and feeling with a trusted adult. There are even specialized gender therapists who can offer counsel and help you to unpack how you're feeling. Acknowledging you are transgender can be a scary step, especially if the idea is new to you, but it can also be a very freeing step as you realize you are not alone. There are plenty of other transgender people out there, and many of them may have experienced some of the same things that you have.

CHAPTER 2

MENTAL AND EMOTIONAL HEALTH

Being a teenager is hard. It is an emotional roller coaster regardless of your gender identity. Bullying is unfortunately common. Hormones are raging, and your body is undergoing changes. For transgender teens, many of these circumstances are heightened. Bullying is more frequent, as kids have a tendency to lash out at ideas and people that they don't understand or that are different from what they are used to. Hormones and changing bodies can likewise lead to extra body discomfort for transgender teens. In Jessy's case, his changing body created a lot of anxiety and confusion. He knew he was a man, but his body was showing signs of a woman going through puberty. The extra stress placed on transgender teens can lead to mental and emotional health issues.

TELLING THE TRUTH

Created by the Transgender Law Center and Gay-Straight Alliance Network, TRUTH is a national storytelling campaign created so that transgender and gender nonconforming teens can share their personal experiences. The movement aims to build empathy and understanding while also providing young people with an important outlet for revealing their stories.

One teen who chose to tell his story is high school senior Ashton. He explains that he knew he was gender nonconforming at a young age. When his elementary school teacher would divide the classroom into boys and girls, he felt uncomfortable and not sure which side he belonged on. By researching on the Internet in his teens, he was able to figure out a word for what he felt: transgender. He came out as transgender to his parents. When he grows up, he wants to work with organizations that help other transgender people.

Ashton's story is one of many in the TRUTH campaign. You can watch more stories about the lives of transgender teens at http://transgenderlawcenter.org/programs/truth.

STRESS AND ITS EFFECTS

One of the major causes of stress for transgender people and those who don't conform to gender norms comes from the way they are treated by society. Gender nonconformity carries a stigma in many cultures around the world, and this stigma can lead to what is called "minority stress." This is stress experienced by any stigmatized minority group. As an effect of discrimination and bias, transgender people may have limited access to social support systems and a lower socioeconomic status. Both of these problems are disproportionately found in transgender communities and are causes of stress. Such stress is made worse by prejudice, abuse, and neglect, especially when it comes from a transgender person's family and peers. Being exposed to stress and stigma repeatedly over a long period of time can lead to many health issues.

Anxiety and depression are two results of stress that affect the transgender community. These problems are worse for those who are prevented from expressing their gender identity or for those lacking a strong support network from family and community. Depression and anxiety can lead to a number of other health issues. One such issue is tobacco use, which is very common in the transgender population and which can lead to heart and lung problems. Transgender communities also have higher rates of drug and alcohol abuse, because people use drugs and alcohol as a coping mechanism. Addiction to drugs and alcohol can themselves lead to a host of health problems including potential for overdose as well as long-term wear on the body. Alcohol and drug use are also connected to high-risk sexual behaviors that can lead to acquiring sexually transmitted diseases and infections, including HIV. HIV—human immunodeficiency virus—leads to AIDS, or acquired immune deficiency syndrome. According to the Centers for Disease Control (CDC), members of the transgender community in the United States have one of the highest risks for HIV infection. Transgender youth are also most

Kassidy was rejected by her family when she came out as transgender at seventeen. She had problems with drugs and homelessness, but found a supportive home through an organization called Project SAFE.

likely to run away from home and drop out of school. Both of these circumstances are usually a direct result of how transgender teens are treated in their home life or at school.

Depression and anxiety are also connected with higher rates of suicide. The 2011 National Transgender Discrimination Survey (NTDS) found that in the United States, 41 percent of transgender and gender nonconforming people had attempted suicide at some point in their lives. Compare this to the national average of 1.6 percent. A 2015 study by researchers at Western

University in London, Ontario, found that the higher suicide rate was directly related to the amount of support—or lack of support—a transgender person received from people around them. The study surveyed over 400 transgender people about their circumstances, their emotional state, and suicidal thoughts. Overall, the survey found that having supportive parents reduced a transgender person's chance of suicidal thoughts or attempted suicide by half. Suicidal thoughts were also reduced when transgender people were able to get legal support for their identity, such as changing their birth certificate to the correct gender. Not surprisingly, those who experienced less transphobia and abuse were also found to be 66 percent less likely to consider suicide. What the study indicates is that much of the stress that affects transgender people comes not internally, but rather from the cisgender world around them.

VIOLENCE AGAINST TRANSGENDER PEOPLE

Transgender people, and particularly transgender women, are at greater risk for assault, rape, and murder. Studies indicate that as many as 50 percent of transgender people will be sexually assaulted in their lifetime. This is a staggering statistic. Worse still, many transgender people feel that they cannot trust support systems that cisgender people usually turn to in situations of crisis: police, schools, and health care workers. According to the National Transgender Discrimination Survey, 22 to 38 percent of transgender people have been harassed by police and more than 15 percent experienced physical abuse from police. Likewise, 26 percent of transgender people reported experiencing violence at the hands of health care professionals. Also, 78 percent of

Protesters from several local organizations in Washington, DC, rallied for better treatment of the transgender community by police and other legal authorities at this 2011 protest.

transgender youth reported experiencing discrimination at schools, while 31 percent experienced this discrimination from teachers.

These statistics are heartbreaking and are a black mark on our society. When people in positions of power misuse that power, they break the trust their communities have placed in them. For a transgender youth, it also shows the importance of building a strong support network of people you can trust. If you feel a teacher is treating you or another transgender student unfairly, find another adult at your school, such as a supportive teacher or counselor, who takes the situation seriously. If you have been assaulted or harassed by anyone, including someone in a position of authority, don't let them silence or isolate you. Find an adult you trust and explain the situation. You can also reach out to local LGBTQ organizations or, if there are none near you, national hotlines. Trans Lifeline is one example. They can be reached online (http://www.translifeline.org) or by phone in both the United States and Canada.

FINDING SOLUTIONS

Since many of the emotional and mental health issues affecting transgender communities come from the outside world, how are

Therapy can help transgender youth unpack issues around their gender identity and society's response to it. Here a therapist at the Transgender Institute in Kansas City, Missouri, speaks to a transgender teen.

transgender people supposed to combat them? Transgender people should seek out a counselor or therapist trained in transgender issues if they are feeling depressed, anxious, or experiencing suicidal thoughts. It is also important to surround yourself with positive people who are accepting of you. If you have trouble finding people in your area, reach out to LGBTQ community and education centers that can provide support and assistance even from far away.

To truly improve the mental and emotional health of people who are transgender, society has to change in some big ways. This can only happen through public education and policy advocacy aimed at ending transphobia and stigma against transgender people. Another important step would be introducing better training for community agencies and services so that they are able to provide helpful and unbiased care to transgender people. These include police, social services, education, health care, and more. Real change can come, but much of that change has to come with the way society views transgender people.

CHAPTER 3

GENDER DYSPHORIA

A cisnormative society and transphobia do create a great deal of stress for transgender people. However, not all of the stress that transgender people experience comes from the outside world. Some of the discomfort, frustration, and confusion that lead to serious emotional and mental health issues comes from within. Feeling that your body does not match your identity can lead to a strong desire for your body to change. This desire can rise to the point of an emotional need. Not having these needs met can lead to greater dissatisfaction and stress. This dissatisfaction and discomfort can reach levels at which it is hard to function in everyday life, such as in school, at work, or while hanging out with friends.

For situations in which the stress of a having a body that does not match one's gender identity is great enough that it requires medical intervention, health care professionals created the term "gender dysphoria." "Dysphoria" comes from the Greek word *dysphoros* meaning "difficult to bear." The word

A diagnosis of gender dysphoria can occur at any age. Sue Pascoe was diagnosed at age fifty-five. She got gender reaffirmation surgery in 2015 and now speaks out about helping other transgender people.

means a feeling of profound dissatisfaction with life. It is the opposite of the word "euphoria," which means "a feeling of extreme happiness and satisfaction."

It is important to note that while many transgender people experience gender dysphoria, not all transgender people do. Furthermore, not all transgender people require medical intervention or treatment. Some transgender people may choose to express their gender identity in other ways and are perfectly comfortable with their bodies as they exist. They may take other steps, such as cutting their hair or dressing to match their gender identity. Or they may choose a different name and ask to be called by pronouns that better fit their identities.

GENDER DYSPHORIA IN THE *DSM*

Gender dysphoria is a condition listed in the *Diagnostic and Statistical Manual of Mental Disorders* (*DSM*). The *DSM* is a manual published by the American Psychiatric Association. This reference manual catalogues different disorders and conditions and lists the criteria for diagnosing them. It is referenced by doctors, researchers, health insurance companies, government policy makers, and the legal system. The *DSM* is updated as new information becomes available and as ideas change. It is now in its fifth edition, known as the *DSM-5*. *DSM-5* categorizes people with gender dysphoria as "people whose gender at birth is contrary to the one they identify with."

As people have learned more about gender identity and what it means to be transgender, the definitions in the *DSM* have changed. Originally, gender dysphoria was known as gender identity disorder. The term "gender identity disorder" was first added in *DSM-3* back in 1980. Many people felt that the term "gender identity disorder" encouraged the idea that being transgender was wrong and that it was a disorder that needed to be fixed. Transgender people are not the only ones who have found themselves pathologized over the years. The *DSM* has added and removed many different conditions and disorders that they now realize are non-medical. For example, homosexuality was considered a disorder until the *DSM-II* was reprinted in 1974 to remove it. Gender identity disorder remained under that name until *DSM-5* was published in 2013. Previously, gender identity

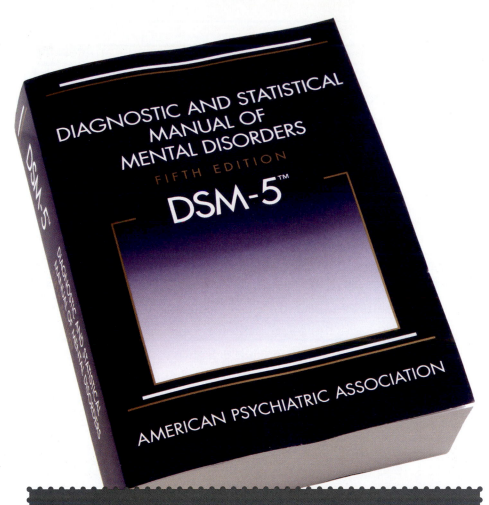

The *DSM-5* was published by the American Psychiatric Association in 2013. Its inclusion of gender dysphoria met with a mixed reaction in the transgender community.

disorder was categorized in the *DSM* under sexual disorders. In *DSM-5*, not only has the name changed to gender dysphoria, but the term has also been moved to its own category in the manual.

While there is still a long way to go, acceptance of transgender people—and people who identity as gender nonbinary, in particular—is growing over the years. This is especially true in how transgender people are seen by the health care and

HOW TRANSGENDER PEOPLE ARE VIEWED AROUND THE WORLD

Being transgender is nothing new. People around the world and throughout history have had similar gender experiences, and some cultures are less rigid about forcing people into a gender binary. For example, several First Nations groups in North America have long recognized the existence of more than two genders. These include the Lakota and Zuni peoples. In Samoan culture, transgender women have a special role in society.

Beyond cultural significance, there are also several countries that have made strides in the legal recognition of more than two gender options. In 2014, Australian courts ruled to allow for a third gender nonspecific option for birth certificates. Australia was the sixth country to officially allow for a third gender distinction. Many of these countries are in the eastern hemisphere, including Nepal, India, Pakistan, and New Zealand. In Nepal, it is possible to have a third gender on your passport for traveling internationally. In 2013, Germany became the first European country to allow a third gender category on birth certificates. Allowing for a third gender option on birth certificates is an extremely important step. For one thing, if an infant is born and doctors aren't sure of the gender, they may choose one—and they may choose wrong.

psychological community. It is fair to say we are at a turning point in how transgender people and gender identity are viewed.

PSYCHOLOGICAL APPROACHES TO TRANSGENDER CARE

The *DSM-5* makes very clear that being transgender is NOT a mental disorder. What may require treatment is the physical and mental distress that often accompanies having a gender identity at odds with one's body. These symptoms can include stress, anxiety, and depression. The *DSM-5* advises treatment focused on helping to relieve the stress. Trying to convince someone they are wrong about their gender identity is never an acceptable treatment. In 2015, the American Psychological Association (APA) released a series of sixteen "Guidelines for Psychological Practice with Transgender and Gender Nonconforming People." According to the APA, these are intended to address "lifespan development, stigma, discrimination and barriers to care faced by this population."

So if being transgender or gender nonconforming is not a disorder to be fixed, then why is it in the *DSM-5?* The reason given is simple: because the conditions caused by gender dysphoria can be alleviated with treatment. Accessing medical care and treatments is difficult without a diagnosis. Another possible benefit to having gender dysphoria in the *DSM* is that some transgender people find that having a diagnosis helps legitimize their experience.

However, other people think that gender dysphoria should be removed from the *DSM* altogether. While its inclusion does play an important role in helping transgender people get the care they need—and sometimes even makes that care eligible

Finding a doctor who is empathetic and understanding of an individual's particular health issues is important for anyone, but particularly for those in the transgender community.

for health insurance coverage—it may do more harm than good. Pathologizing or medicalizing the transgender experience can add to the stigma people feel about it.

SIGNS OF GENDER DYSPHORIA

The *DSM-5* has many criteria for identifying people suffering from gender dysphoria. In order to receive this diagnosis, the person must experience discomfort with their body, a need to be treated as a gender other than that which society currently assigns to them, and a strong feeling that their physical body does not match their true identity. These feelings must continue for at least six months. For a child to be diagnosed with gender dysphoria, they have to verbalize their feelings of being a different gender than the one they were assigned at birth.

Transgender people are not inherently disordered. When they are diagnosed with gender dysphoria, it is because their feelings about their bodies may be alleviated with treatment. However, it is important to remember that treatment will not affect their overall gender identity.

CHAPTER 4

HORMONE REPLACEMENT THERAPY AND GENDER AFFIRMATION SURGERIES

There are a number of medical treatments for gender dysphoria. It should be restated that these treatments are not for the condition of being transgender, but for the stress that being transgender can cause. These methods can help change a transgender person's body so that it matches the person's gender identity. No one treatment is right for all transgender people. Patients should discuss possible treatments with a health care professional to figure out which one is right for them. Some transgender people chose to undergo hormone replacement therapies (HRTs), also known as cross-sex hormones. This means taking hormones that their bodies don't produce on their own. Transgender people can also decide to undergo gender affirmation surgeries.

UNDERSTANDING HORMONES

What exactly are hormones, and what role do they play in the body? The body produces a number of hormones, which are

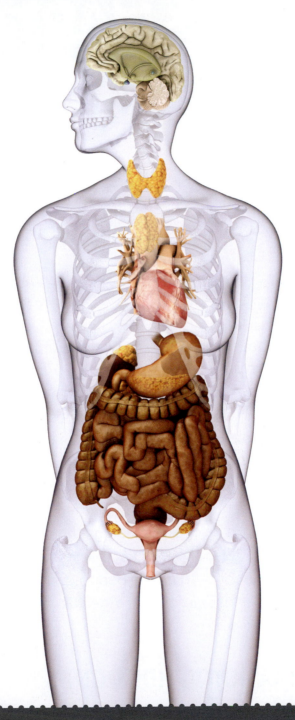

The glands that make up the endocrine system produce and release hormones to regulate metabolism, growth, reproduction, and more. The pancreas, ovaries, testes, and intestinal tract are also part of the system.

chemical messengers that travel through the body and cause body tissues and organs to behave in certain ways. They are controlled by the endocrine system, which consists of a number of hormone-producing glands. The endocrine system and the hormones it produces affect people's growth and development, metabolism, reproduction, and mood. It takes only a small amount of a key hormone to have a big effect on the body.

The main sex hormones are androgens (such as testosterone) and estrogen. People of all genders produce both estrogen and testosterone in their bodies. Some produce more estrogen, while others produce more testosterone. The production of testosterone in a fetus leads to the development of a penis and testicles. Lower levels of testosterone at this stage lead to the development of a labia, uterus, and vagina. Babies are assigned genders at birth based on these secondary sex characteristics, although their assigned genders may not reflect their gender identities. Sex hormones also signal the body to make changes during puberty. Androgens cause a deepening of the voice, a growth spurt, and the growth of both facial hair and pubic hair. Estrogen causes the growth of breasts, filling out of the hips and thighs, and start of menstruation. After puberty, these hormones continue to play a role, including with reproduction and general health.

HORMONE REPLACEMENT

Hormone replacement therapies (HRTs) in transgender people involve administering sex hormones and suppressing others as a way to help the person's secondary sex characteristics match their gender identity. Transgender women can take hormone blockers to suppress their testosterone. They can also take

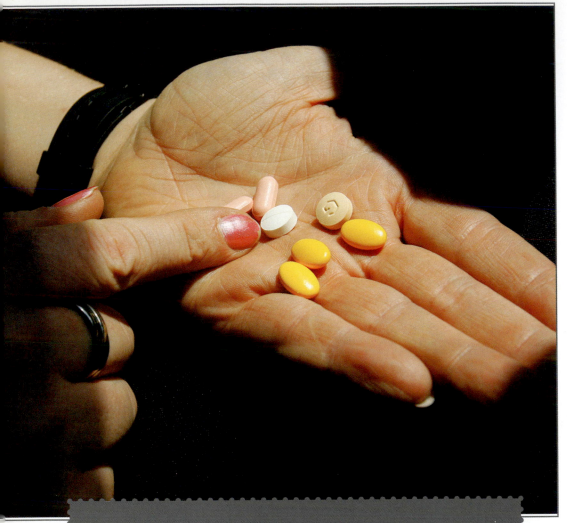

A transgender Kansas police officer shows the hormones she takes daily to help keep her body matching her gender identity.

estrogen. These can have several feminizing effects on the body. The genitals may reduce in size. Fat may be distributed more about the hips and muscles may become smaller. Breasts may form. Facial hair and body hair may lessen. On the other hand, transgender men can take testosterone, which can lead to masculine features. It can lead to body and facial hair growth, increased muscle mass, and a deeper voice. It will also often cause the man to stop having periods. Some transgender men also develop acne as a side effect of taking estrogen.

Individuals will respond to hormone replacement therapies differently. It's also important to know that results do not happen overnight. It takes several years to see the full effects of the hormones. Once a person starts taking the hormones, they have to take them for the rest of their life. If they stop taking the hormones, then their body will pretty much return to the way it was before. However, some of the changes may be irreversible.

There are several different ways to administer HRTs. These include injections, pills, and patches that are applied to the skin and slowly release hormones into the bloodstream. Again, no one method is better than others. A doctor's advice can provide the method that is best for each individual's needs.

RISKS AND SIDE EFFECTS

The hormones that are taken as part of HRTs are considered reasonably safe. They are very similar to the natural hormones your body produces. Few people experience major side effects as a result of taking hormones. However, it is important to be aware of these side effects, even if they are rare. Taking estrogen changes the way the body stores and processes fat. This can cause fat to build up around the organs, which some doctors believe can lead to higher rates of diabetes and heart disease. In a 2014 study on the effects of HRTs, only 3.2 percent of the 1,073 transgender women who underwent HRTs had developed type 2 diabetes. The most serious side effects for people taking estrogens are high blood pressure, stroke, and altered liver function. The most serious side effects for people taking testosterone include high cholesterol, blood clots, and diabetes.

While artificial hormones are relatively safe, it is extremely important that they be taken only with a doctor's advice. Never take any drugs or medical treatments that you find on the Internet. First of all, there is no way to verify that the hormones are what they claim to be. They could be a waste of money and have no effect. They could also have negative effects. Without a doctor's advice, you won't know which medications and supplements are safe to mix with hormones, or if you are mentally and physically prepared to begin a treatment. It can be frustrating waiting for a doctor's help. It can also be tempting to try to solve a problem by yourself without adult involvement. No matter how tempting they are, never give in to buying or taking hormones off the Internet without a doctor's help.

Here are a few more tips to help make taking HRTs a positive and safe experience:

- Find a health care provider you can trust. Be honest with your doctor about how you are feeling and if you have any concerns or are experiencing any side effects.
- Do your own research, stay informed, and don't be afraid to ask questions if you don't understand what your doctor is saying.
- Don't take a higher hormone dosage than you are prescribed. It won't speed up the effects on your body and may even slow them down.
- Remember that while HRTs may help, they are only part of a positive quality of life. Surround yourself with supportive friends and family. A good support system goes a long way to helping overall health.

WHEN DO YOU START TAKING HORMONES?

For transgender people who have already gone through puberty, the changes caused by HRTs will alter some but not all aspects of their physical body. During puberty, increased levels of androgens cause people to develop deeper voices, increased muscle mass, and more body hair, and even their bones change as they become taller. So for example, a transgender woman undergoing HRTs after puberty may always be taller than the average woman. The shape of the skull and face are also cemented during puberty and are less likely to change after it without surgery.

Many transgender people are aware of their gender identity early in life, sometimes in toddlerhood or early childhood. They may experience gender dysphoria in early adolescence and especially around the onset of puberty. There are treatment options that can help transgender adolescents. Once gender dysphoria is diagnosed, doctors can prescribe something called pubertal suppression or puberty-blocking drugs. This is accomplished in adolescents through the use of a gonadotropin-releasing hormone analogue. It essentially keeps puberty from happening. In a transgender girl, this can prevent an Adam's apple from forming or facial hair growth from occurring. Pubertal suppression is reversible. This allows adolescents to avoid the discomfort of puberty while developing their feelings about their gender identity and making decisions. Pubertal suppression can potentially decrease stress in transgender adolescents. Once they've firmly decided they would like to affirm their gender identity in more permanent ways, they can then begin taking

Many transgender kids realize and affirm their gender identity long before puberty. This photo shows seven-year-old Tyler, who began expressing to his parents that he was a boy at age two.

hormones. Depending on the person and their situation, this process may begin in the teens. Puberty-blocking hormones can make future transition safer and easier. Alternatively, if they decide for whatever reason to allow their body to develop without HRTs, they can stop taking the puberty-blocking hormones with no harm done.

Studies into the effects of pubertal suppression are just beginning. In a 2014 study on the effects of pubertal suppression

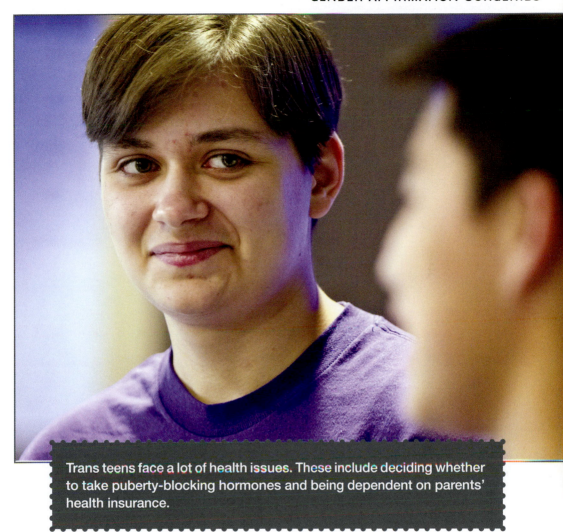

Trans teens face a lot of health issues. These include deciding whether to take puberty-blocking hormones and being dependent on parents' health insurance.

on transgender teens, researchers determined that the well-being of people who had been prescribed puberty-blocking drugs and later undergone gender-affirmation surgeries was similar to the well-being of people in the general cisgender population in a similar age bracket. Overall, the results of the study were hopeful and suggest that puberty-blocking drugs might be a good way for transgender people to avoid the negative effects of gender dysphoria.

In 2016, the United States National Institutes of Health (NIH) announced it would begin a $5.7 million project to study the psychological effects of delaying puberty in transgender teens. The researchers said they hope to study 280 adolescents who identify as transgender. While half of the participants in the study are receiving puberty-blocking drugs, the other half will receive HRTs only after having gone through puberty. Researchers plan to study both groups over the course of five years to get a better idea of the long-term effects of pubertal

PUBERTY

The changes that happen in your body when you take hormones are similar to the changes that occur during puberty. Puberty is the stage of development when a child turns into an adult capable of reproduction. During puberty, a person's body will grow and change very rapidly. The only other period in which a person's body grows and changes as rapidly is when that person is a baby.

Puberty is a stage that actually is itself divided into several stages. These are called Tanner stages, and they were developed by a British doctor and professor named James M. Tanner. There are five different Tanner stages, each with their own developmental milestones for things like height, pubic hair, and the development of other secondary sex characteristics.

suppression on health and well-being. In 2012, the American Academy of Child and Adolescent Psychiatry supported best practices for transgender preteens beginning puberty-blocking drugs to allow more time to explore their feelings without going through the trauma of puberty.

GENDER AFFIRMATION SURGERIES

In addition to HRTs, some transgender people choose to get surgeries. This can be a way to alter their bodies to further match their gender identity. Gender affirmation surgeries are just that: a way to affirm a person's true gender. These procedures are sometimes referred to in the medical community by the term "sex reassignment surgery" or "SRS." They may also be called gender reassignment surgeries or gender confirmation surgeries.

Before we look at what gender affirmation surgeries are, we first must go over what they are not. First, they are not a requirement for being transgender. Not all transgender people choose to get surgeries. Choosing to not undergo surgery does not impact one's gender identity or make one's gender experience any less real. Second, gender affirmation surgeries are not a cosmetic surgery. While both gender affirmation surgeries and cosmetic surgeries alter the body and make it look different, gender affirmation surgeries are a medical need for those that undergo them. Gender affirmation surgery can be a treatment for those who suffer from gender dysphoria.

Gender affirmation surgeries cover a wide range of procedures. For transgender men, these may include having a mastectomy (removing of the breasts) and phalloplasty and scrotoplasty (both altering the genitals to masculinize them). For transgender women, surgeries may include breast implants

Atticus Ranck of Florida came out as transgender as a teen and has since used hormones and undergone surgery to help his body match his gender identity.

and a vaginoplasty (altering the genitals to feminize them). Some transgender women may choose to undergo facial surgeries to further feminize their features, such as a tracheal shave to remove an Adam's apple. Like any surgeries, these procedures come with risks and recovery time. As with HRTs or any treatment plan, it's important to find a health care provider whose expertise and opinion you trust and ask plenty of questions to find out what path is right for you and your body.

CHAPTER 5

THE PURSUIT OF HEALTH AND HAPPINESS

Transgender people will have unique health issues throughout their lives. If they choose to undergo HRTs and/or surgeries, they will be taking hormones regularly for the rest of their lives. They may also face greater obstacles to receiving proper health care as a result of a cisnormative health care system.

Transgender people also need to be aware of gender-specific conditions they may be at risk for. For example, transgender men are still at risk for cancers of the uterus, breast, and ovaries, provided they still have these organs. Transgender women have a low risk of prostate cancer, but they should still be screened for it.

HEALTH INSURANCE ISSUES

Getting access to health care has long been an issue for transgender people. They can face a number of hurdles, such as health care workers who are unfamiliar with transgender health needs or who are biased against them. They may also have difficulty accessing or relying on adequate health insurance. This is in part because transgender communities experience higher rates of unemployment and poverty. A major reason for this is because of the prejudice, biases, and difficulties of navigating a cisnormative world as a transgender person.

Additionally, transgender people who do have access to health insurance often have difficulty getting necessary procedures covered. This doesn't just apply to the coverage of feminizing and masculinizing hormones or gender-affirmation surgeries, but also to other health care procedures. For example, say a transgender man develops a condition that health care providers associate with women, such as uterine fibroids. These non-cancerous growths that develop on the uterus are more common later in life. Uterine fibroids can be treated with a hysterectomy. However, if a transgender man is listed in his insurance as male, he may not be considered eligible for a hysterectomy. The expensive surgery may not be covered. This is another way in which a cisnormative society can work against transgender people.

There are some government acts that offer protections for transgender people's health care. The Affordable Care Act was passed in 2010. It includes a number of provisions to make it harder for health insurance companies to deny coverage to transgender people. One of these provisions states that hospitals and health care facilities that are receiving federal financial resources cannot discriminate against people based on gender or sexuality. This provision has been interpreted by courts and the Department of Health and Human Services as also preventing discrimination against people who are transgender or gender nonconforming. This is an important step forward as, according

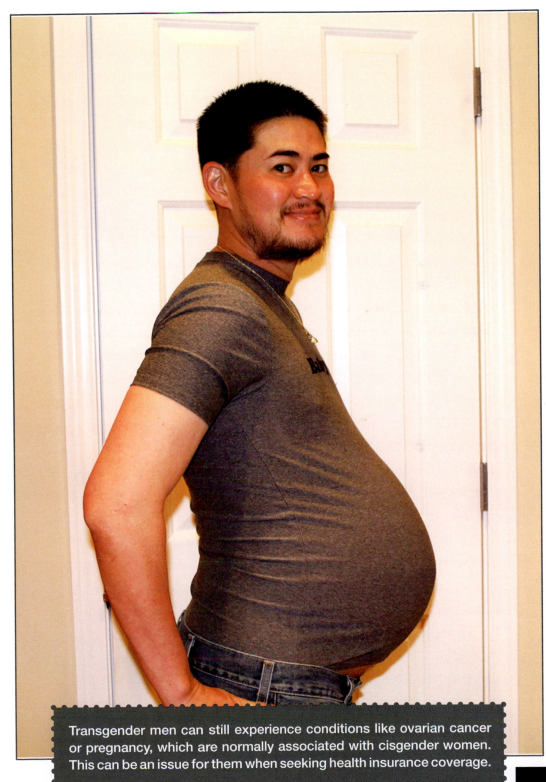

Transgender men can still experience conditions like ovarian cancer or pregnancy, which are normally associated with cisgender women. This can be an issue for them when seeking health insurance coverage.

to the National Transgender Discrimination Survey, nearly one in five transgender people reported having been refused health care. More than one in four reported having been harassed while seeking health care. This can lead to transgender people not seeking out care when they are ill for fear of discrimination. The Affordable Care Act also makes it illegal for health insurance companies to refuse to cover people who have "pre-existing conditions," which include transgender dysphoria.

While there are laws in place to help stop discrimination by health care providers and health insurance companies, there are no national laws that require health insurance companies to cover important treatments like HRTs and gender affirmation surgeries. By 2016, only five states in the United States required health insurance providers to cover the treatments related to transition. Those states were California, Colorado, Connecticut, Oregon, and Vermont. Oregon was the only state that also required coverage of pubertal suppression or puberty blockers. In Canada, many jurisdictions publicly fund gender affirmation surgeries. However, there are still barriers to people actually accessing this care. Few Canadian health care facilities offer the surgeries, creating bottlenecks to receiving care. Transgender people may have to remain on a long wait list for years before getting the surgery they need. There is hope that in the future more governments will move in the direction of requiring funding and increasing the availability of health care for transgender people.

THERE'S AN APP FOR THAT

There are many applications designed specifically to help transgender people on their journey through therapeutic

Technology is helping to make accessing transgender health information easier. Apps like MyTransHealth can be reached on a smartphone or tablet.

treatment, HRTs, and gender affirmation surgeries. MyTransHealth is one example. It's an app that was built to help transgender people find transgender-friendly health care options. "We built four different categories into MyTransHealth: medical, legal, mental health, and crisis," said its creator in an interview with the *Daily Dot*. "And once you delve into those categories you can still filter down through different needs, like wheelchair accessibility, insurance coverage, or language."

The creators of the MyTransHealth app say that they saw the need for it because of the difficulties transgender people have in finding knowledgeable health care options to address their needs. This app and its accompanying website received substantial support and crowd funding. The app launched in May 2016.

HELP FROM HOTT

There are a number of programs and organizations that help transgender people. Some of them are specifically for transgender teens. One of these is Health Outreach to Teens (HOTT). HOTT is a Manhattan-based, confidential, youth-only center. It offers health care to LGBTQ adolescents. These services are provided free of charge or for a low cost. Some of these services include:

- General medical care
- Gynecological exams/reproductive health
- Testing and treatment for sexually transmitted infections
- Cross-gender hormone therapy or HRTs
- Individual counseling and support groups

Having treatment centers especially for the LGBTQ community is an important part of having inclusive health care.

Another app, TransLog, can be used for keeping a journal, or log, of body changes during the transition process. The application can be downloaded and works on Windows systems. It can help transgender people track their medication and physical progress. Keeping track of small changes and milestones can be a beneficial part of the process.

THE FUTURE OF TRANSGENDER HEALTH CARE

Transgender health care has come a long way. While a lot of prejudice still exists, health care is moving in the right direction and becoming better able to serve transgender communities. It was only in 2007 that the first clinic was opened to treat transgender children, the Gender Management Service in Boston's Children's Hospital. Pediatric endocrinologists at the hospital help transgender children and their guardians choose a proper course of treatment. In 2011, the Center of Excellence for Transgender Health published protocols for health care workers to help understand transgender health care. In 2012, Beth Scott, a transgender woman, won a court case that argued that her mammogram should be covered by her insurance carrier, Aetna. A 2014 court case won by a transgender woman, Denee Mallon, said that people receiving Medicare cannot be automatically denied coverage for a gender affirmation surgery. And in 2016, the United States Department of Health and Human Services ruled that transgender people are entitled to gender affirming surgeries provided by Medicare Advantage insurers.

These victories were won thanks to the efforts of many brave transgender people who didn't give up when the deck was stacked against them. One day, it will hopefully not be so difficult. People will come to accept that transgender people are not that different from cisgender people. Transgender people might always have some unique health needs that will require understanding. But everyone—regardless of their gender identity or any other characteristic of their identity—deserves basic human rights. We all have the right to pursue happiness, which often goes hand in hand with the equally important pursuit of health.

GLOSSARY

ADVOCACY Working to build support for a cause or group.

CISGENDER Having a gender identity that matches the gender assigned at birth.

ENDOCRINE SYSTEM A system in the body that produces and regulates hormones.

GENDER AFFIRMATION SURGERY A procedure to alter the body of a transgender person to help it fit the person's gender identity.

GENDER BINARY The idea that every person is either a man or a woman.

GENDER EXPRESSION The ways—such as hairstyle, clothing, and behavior—in which a person expresses their gender.

GENDER IDENTITY A person's internal sense of being a man, woman, both, or neither.

HORMONE A chemical messenger in the body.

HORMONE REPLACEMENT THERAPY (HRT) The prescribed use of hormones with the intention of changing a transgender person's secondary sex characteristics.

HYSTERECTOMY A surgery to remove the uterus, or womb.

MAMMOGRAM An X-ray screening to check for breast cancer.

MASTECTOMY The surgical removal of breasts.

MINORITY STRESS Pressure or tension placed on stigmatized minority groups.

PATHOLOGIZE To treat something as abnormal or unhealthy.

PUBERTY A stage of development when a child becomes an adult capable of reproduction.

SEXUALITY People's gender preference in terms of with whom they are attracted to or want to form relationships. Heterosexual, homosexual (gay and lesbian), and bisexual are all sexualities.

SOCIOECONOMIC Relating to a person's status in the world, based on their income, education level, and other factors.

STIGMA A feeling of disgrace associated with a particular group, action, or circumstance.

STROKE A loss of consciousness caused by the oxygen being cut off to the brain.

TRANSGENDER Having a gender identity that does not match that assigned at birth.

TRANSPHOBIA Prejudice against transgender people.

FOR MORE INFORMATION

American Congress of Obstetricians and Gynecologists

409 12th Street SW

Washington, DC 20024

(800) 673-8444

Website: http://www.acog.org

This professional and educational organization is focused on obstetrics and gynecology. It maintains a transgender health resource guide with helpful links for both health care providers and patients.

American Psychiatric Association

1000 Wilson Boulevard, Suite 1825

Arlington, VA 22209

(888) 357-7924

Website: https://www.psychiatry.org

The Psychiatric Association is a professional organization for psychiatrists in the United States. The organization maintains and updates the *Diagnostic and Statistical Manual of Mental Disorders (DSM)*.

American Psychological Association (APA)

750 First Street NE

Washington, DC 20002

(800) 374-2721

Website: http://www.apa.org

The American Psychological Association is a leading scientific and professional organization devoted to advancing the research of psychologists and psychological knowledge. In

2015, they released a series of best practice guidelines for health care professionals working with transgender patients.

Canadian Professional Association for Transgender Health (CPATH)
Sherbourne Health Centre
333 Sherbourne Street
Toronto, ON M5A 2S5
Canada
(416) 324-4100
Website: http://www.rainbowhealthontario.ca
CPATH is a professional organization focused on transgender health care. They operate Trans Health Connection, a project to improve transgender health care in Ontario through training, education, mentorship, resources, and networking.

Endocrine Society
2055 L Street NW, Suite 600
Washington, DC 20036
(888) 363-6274 Website: https://www.endocrine.org
This is a professional organization focused on hormone research and the clinical practice of endocrinology. The organization has published clinical guidelines for treating transgender people that make recommendations on diagnostic procedures, treatment of adolescents, hormonal treatment and monitoring, and screening guidelines.

National Center for Transgender Equality (NCTE)
1400 16th Street NW, Suite 510
Washington, DC 20036
(202) 642-4542

Website: http://www.transequality.org
NCTE work to pass local, state, and federal laws and policies to
    better the lives of transgender people. Their website includes
    a great deal of information about health care and other issues
    facing transgender people.

WEBSITES

Because of the changing nature of internet links, Rosen Publishing
has developed an online list of websites related to the subject of
this book. This site is updated regularly. Please use this link to
access the list:

http://www.rosenlinks.com/TL/health

FOR FURTHER READING

Andrews, Arin. *Some Assembly Required: The Not-So-Secret Life of a Transgender Teen.* New York, NY: Simon & Schuster, 2014.

Beam, Cris. *I Am J.* New York, NY: Hachette Book Group, 2011.

Erickson-Schroth, Laura. *Trans Bodies, Trans Selves: A Resource for the Transgender Community.* New York, NY: Oxford University Press, 2014.

Foss, Sonja K., and Mary E. Domenico. *Gender Selves: Negotiating Identity in a Binary World.* Long Grove, IL: Waveland Press, 2012.

Garbacik, Jamiee. *Gender & Sexuality for Beginners.* Danbury, CT: For Beginners LLC, 2013.

Gromko, Linda. *Where's MY Book? A Guide for Transgender and Gender Non-Conforming Youth, Their Parents, & Everyone Else.* Bainbridge Island, WA: Bainbridge Books, 2015.

Huegel, Kelly. *GLBTQ: The Survival Guide for Gay, Lesbian, Bisexual, Transgender, and Questioning Teens.* Golden Valley, MN: Free Spirit Publishing, 2011.

Nutt, Amy Ellis. *Becoming Nicole: The Transformation of an American Family.* New York, NY: Random House, 2015.

Pepper, Rachel. *Transitions of the Heart: Stories of Love, Struggle, and Acceptance by Mothers of Transgender and Gender Variant Children.* San Francisco, CA: Cleris Press, 2012.

Polonsky, Ami. *Gracefully Grayson.* New York, NY: Hyperion, 2014.

Teich, Nicholas M. *Transgender 101: A Simple Guide to a Complex Issue.* New York, NY: Columbia University Press, 2012.

Testa, Rylan Jay, and Deborah Coolhart. *The Gender Quest Workbook: A Guide for Teens and Young Adults Exploring Gender Identity.* Oakland, CA: Raincoast Books, 2015.

BIBLIOGRAPHY

American Psychological Association. *Diagnostic and Statistical Manual of Mental Disorders.* 5th ed. Washington, DC: American Psychological Association, 2013.

Boghani, Priyanka. "When Transgender Kids Transition, Medical Risks Are Both Known and Unknown." *PBS*, June 30, 2015 (http://www.pbs.org/wgbh/frontline/article/when -transgender-kids-transition-medical-risks-are-both-known -and-unknown/).

Brill, Stephanie A. *The Transgender Child: A Handbook for Families and Professionals.* San Francisco, CA: Cleris Press, 2008.

Eckstrand, Kristen L., and Jesse M. Ehrenfeld. *Lesbian, Gay, Bisexual, and Transgender Healthcare: A Clinical Guide to Preventive, Primary, and Specialist Care.* New York, NY: Springer Publishing, 2016.

Ehrensaft, Diane, and Edgardo Menvielle. *Gender Born, Gender Made: Raising Healthy Gender-Nonconforming Children.* New York, NY: The Experiment, 2011.

Erickson-Schroth, Laura. *Trans Bodies, Trans Selves: A Resource for the Transgender Community.* New York, NY: Oxford University Press, 2014.

"Healthcare Rights of Transgender People." National Center for Transgender Equality, March 15, 2016 (http://www .transequality.org/sites/default/files/docs/kyr/KYR -Healthcare-May-2016.pdf).

Kuklin, Susan. *Beyond Magenta: Transgender Teens Speak Out.* Somerville, MA: Candlewick Press, 2014.

Makadon, Harvey J., Kenneth H. Mayer, and Jennifer Potter. *Fenway Guide to Lesbian, Gay, Bisexual, and Transgender*

Health. 2nd Edition. Philadelphia, PA: American College of Physicians, 2015

Reisner, Sari. "Meeting the Health Care Needs of Transgender People." The Fenway Institute. Retrieved June 8, 2016 (http://www.lgbthealtheducation.org/wp-content/uploads/Sari-slides_final1.pdf).

"Transgender Health-AMSA." *AMSA*. Retrieved June 8, 2016 (http://www.amsa.org/advocacy/action-committees/gender-sexuality/transgender-health/).

INDEX

ABOUT THE AUTHOR

Susan Meyer is the author of more than fifteen young adult books. She volunteers at Safe Place, an Austin-based organization that provides safety and healing for survivors of domestic violence and sexual assault and is an open and welcoming provider of resources to the LGBTQ community. The organization also works to change attitudes and policies and improve awareness around these issues. Meyer lives in Austin, Texas, with her husband, Sam, and cat, Dinah.

PHOTO CREDITS

Cover Christophe Archembault/AFP/Getty Images; pp. 5, 8, 15, Leland Bobbe/The Image Bank/Getty Images; p. 10 Adam Hester/ Blend Images/Getty Images; p. 13 Raleigh News & Observer/ Tribune News Service/Getty Images; p. 20, 44 © AP Images; p. 22, 40 The Washington Post/Getty Images; p. 23, 36, 41 Kansas City Star/Tribune News Service/Getty Images; p. 26, 47 Barcroft Media/Getty Images; p. 28 H.S. Photos/Science Source; p. 31 Thomas Barwick/Stone/Getty Images; p. 34 Dorling Kindersley/ Getty Images; p. 49 Stokkete/Shutterstock.com; cover and interior pages background graphic Shutterstock.com.

Designer: Nicole Russo; Editor: Amelie von Zumbusch;
Photo Researcher: Nicole Baker